Behind the Scenes at the Zoo

Written by Nancy O'Connor

Flying Start
to Literacy®

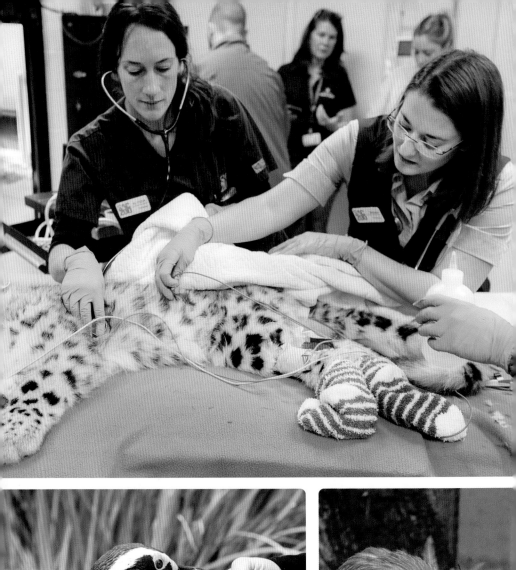

Contents

Introduction

Have you ever spent a day at the zoo?

Zoos are wonderful places to observe birds, reptiles, sea creatures and many other kinds of animals that you rarely get to see.

When you see bears, sea lions or rhinos up close, you can learn how they live and play, what they eat and how they raise their young.

What if you were asked to create a zoo? It is a fun idea to think about, but it's also complicated. What steps are needed to build a zoo from the ground up?

You might say, "Collect some animals." But where are you going to put them? What sorts of things do they eat? Who is going to care for that tiger with an infected claw or the hippo with a tummy ache?

Let's take a look behind the scenes at a zoo.

Chapter 1
Building deserts, jungles and mountains

An **architect** is a person who designs buildings and often supervises their construction. Some architects specialise in building zoo habitats. If you want to create a zoo, you will need an architect. The architect must meet with the keepers, because they understand the needs of their zoo residents.

A mountain goat needs rocky cliffs to climb. A
polar bear needs a pool of icy water where it can
swim and keep cool. Hummingbirds might live
comfortably in a small **aviary**, but eagles, hawks
or condors need huge spaces where they can spread
their wings. Meerkats must dig their burrows in
sand, and gorillas will thrive only in tropical forests.
The architect considers all these things in creating
healthy habitats.

Entertainment

The residents of the zoo need entertainment, too.
For example, chimpanzees like ropes and vines for
climbing and swinging. Koalas love to perch in trees
high above the ground, and leopards like to hide in
tall grass.

Toys like balls, barrels, hanging rings, hammocks and
ladders should be included in many enclosures. Those
things make life more interesting for the animals.

Safety

The architect must also consider safety – for the animals, their keepers and the people who visit the zoo. Having lots of space to roam is important, but no one wants an animal to escape and maybe cause harm.

Tall fences or thick glass surround some enclosures. Others have moats to prevent escapes. Moats must be deep and wide enough to do their job.

Protection

Protecting the creatures is important, too. For example, if a lynx is in a wire cage, there must be a barrier outside the cage to keep people far enough away that they don't put food or other objects through the gaps. A barrier can also keep clever monkeys from reaching out to grab things like cameras, mobile phones or someone's hair.

Part of the zoo experience is watching the animals as they eat, sleep and play. An architect may build viewing platforms, large windows or moving walkways. When animals are housed in darkened enclosures, visitors can watch creatures that are usually active only at night.

Equally important, however, is the comfort of the animals. When they are tired or not feeling well, they need private places in which to sleep, hide or care for their babies. It can be disappointing not to see the tiger or lion during your zoo visit, but their wellbeing matters, too.

Chapter 2
Collecting animals

Once you have the perfect habitats, where are you going to get the animals that live in them?

For hundreds of years, wealthy people collected **exotic animals** for their private enjoyment. Hunters went into jungles, mountains and deserts around the world to capture wildlife.

Sometimes, hunters took young animals from their family groups. People bought the animals they wanted from these hunters.

This brown bear has been imprisoned in a cage.

Trading and lending animals

Today, most of the wildlife in modern zoos comes from other zoos. This is through the trading, giving and lending of animals.

Some animals have been born in zoos for the purpose of being shared. These are called captive breeding programs. Others may have been rescued from private owners who have kept them **illegally**. Some may have been injured in the wild and need to be nursed back to health by zoo veterinarians.

The Guam kingfisher is an endangered species of kingfisher from the island of Guam, in the Pacific Ocean.

Protecting endangered species

Zoos also work together to protect endangered species. For example, one zoo may have a healthy male Guam kingfisher and another may have a female. Because the birds are extinct in the wild, putting a mating pair together to have chicks can help the species survive.

Collecting animals for your zoo will depend on your budget and the types of habitats that your architect has built. You may want a variety of large and small animals, as well as those that live in water, on land or in trees. Big cats, elephants, giraffes, penguins, monkeys and zebras are some of the most popular zoo animals.

What's your favourite zoo creature?

Two-month-old panda cubs in Chengdu, China

Chapter 3
What's for breakfast?

Before your zoo is filled with animals, you must know what to feed them. Emily Schwartz is the **nutritionist** at the Los Angeles County Zoo in the United States. She must make sure all 1,400 animals living there have good food so that they can thrive in captivity. It's a hard job to provide for the different needs of **carnivores**, **herbivores** and **omnivores** – from the smallest bird to the largest gorilla.

Emily Schwartz in the zoo kitchen

The zoo kitchen

Emily's kitchen is similar to a large cafeteria. She works from nine to five, but when she arrives at the zoo kitchen, her helpers have already been there for two hours. Every morning, they must sort through new deliveries of boxes and bags filled with fruits, vegetables and other fresh foods the animals like to eat.

Crickets, mice or worms?

Although the zoo kitchen looks like a regular kitchen, the bins on the shelves are not filled with flour or sugar. The bins may hold mealworms or bits of tropical fruit. In the large freezers, there are tightly sealed plastic bins with stacks of frozen mice, whole chickens, fish and beef bones. The crickets chirping in the background will be breakfast for the lizards and meerkats.

Emily studies each animal's diet in its native habitat. Then she and her helpers try to make recipes to match that diet. Everyone wears gloves during the food preparation. The fruits and vegetables are handled in one area and the meats and fish in another. No one wants the animals to get sick because of spoiled food.

When everything is ready, the food is packaged, labelled and put into bins. Zoo employees use golf carts to deliver the bins to different areas of the zoo.

Interview
Emily Schwartz, Zoo nutritionist

When did you decide to become a zoo nutritionist?

I planned to be a regular veterinarian, but I took a class at university on livestock nutrition. I became fascinated with what animals need to eat to stay healthy.

Before I came here to the zoo, though, I worked for a wildlife rescue organisation. Not many zoos around the country have full-time **nutritionists**, so I'm delighted to be working here.

Emily feeding a sloth at the zoo

The rock hyrax looks something like a big guinea pig, but it is one of the closest living relatives to the elephant.

Which animals in your care are the pickiest eaters?

Our rock hyrax refused to eat turnips, a very common food for them in captivity. It took some experimenting with his diet before I discovered that he loves zucchini.

Kelly, our silverback gorilla, hates grapefruit. He gets very angry if anyone tries to feed it to him. One of our small **primates** is very fussy. For a few days, he loves a certain food and then he refuses to ever eat it again.

Feeding 1,400 animals must be expensive.

Our yearly food budget is over a million dollars. Every week, nearly four thousand kilograms of vegetables and fruits are delivered to the zoo kitchen. One of the most expensive food items is papayas, but many birds love them.

Our carnivores, such as our big cats, eat whole **carcasses** of goats, rabbits and pigs that are specially raised for them.

All sorts of herbivores need branches and leaves to **browse** on – giraffes, rhinos, okapi, gorillas, reindeer, camels and kangaroos. Tree-trimming companies deliver the branches and leaves for these animals to eat.

Weekly grocery list:

Wildlife sanctuary, Port Douglas, Queensland

Here are a few of the items on the wildlife sanctuary's grocery list each week to keep its animals well fed and nourished:

- 50 kilograms of fish
- 50 kilograms of kangaroo mince
- 60 kilograms of seeds
- 320 kilograms of macropod pellets
- 3,000 crickets
- 5,000 mealworms
- 60,000 fly pupae
- 60 kilograms of fresh corn
- 140 kilograms of sweet potato
- 50 kilograms of apples
- 50 kilograms of pears
- 70 kilograms of rockmelon
- 70 kilograms of honeydew melon
- 70 kilograms of pawpaw
- 20 kilograms of grapes

Chapter 4
Zoo medical centre

Your zoo will need expert veterinarians. Their job is as varied as the animals they care for, and no two days are the same.

Swimming lessons

The veterinarians at an American zoo were very excited when a baby hippo named Fiona was born in January 2018. Fiona was, however, born early. She was so small and weak, the zookeepers had to take her away from her mother and care for her in a special nursery. She had to be taught how to swim and dive.

When she was big enough, she was reunited with her parents, and visitors to the zoo may now see Fiona for themselves.

Baby shoes

When a new baby giraffe, Hasani (which means "handsome" in Swahili) arrived at an American zoo in May 2019, the vets discovered he was having trouble standing up and walking. They made special shoes for his back feet. These shoes helped Hasani stand to walk until his muscles became stronger. By the age of two months, he was running around, exploring his enclosure.

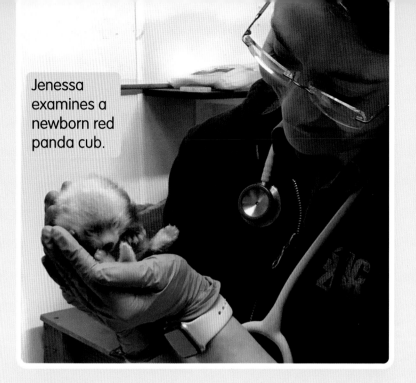

Jenessa examines a newborn red panda cub.

Interview
Jenessa Gjeltema, Zoo veterinarian

Jenessa Gjeltema is the veterinarian at a small zoo that has about 500 animals on six hectares.

She also teaches veterinary medicine at a university that is close to the zoo. The university has a special partnership with the zoo. Students take their classes at the university while gaining practical experience working at the zoo. Not many university programs are designed to train zoo veterinarians.

When did you decide to become a vet?

It was a childhood dream of mine, but when I was at university, I studied international business instead. When I graduated, I realised that wasn't something I was passionate about. However, I loved wildlife and conservation.

So I changed courses and studied to become a zoo vet. I have always wanted to work in a zoo and here I am.

This tiger cub has a sore paw.

Have you had any zoo babies born recently?

A baby red panda named Gizmo was born in July 2019. We're delighted to have him because red pandas are endangered and only 50 per cent survive their first year.

We also have a young snow leopard named Coconut. He had a condition at birth called swimmer's syndrome, and his back leg muscles were very weak. The zoo staff took special care of him. He also had to have eyelid surgery when he was about nine months old, but he is doing great now.

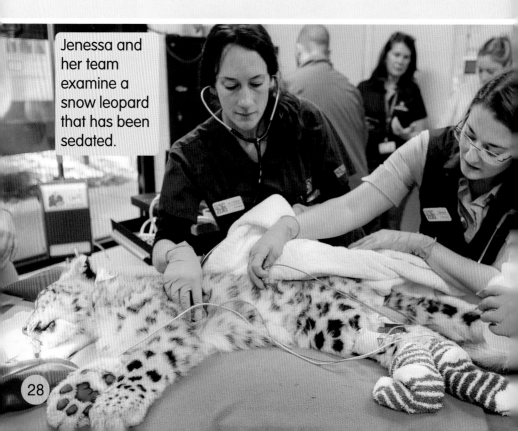

Jenessa and her team examine a snow leopard that has been sedated.

A vet examines a raccoon.

What type of vet care do you provide for the zoo's animals?

I mostly do preventive health exams. We check all our animals regularly, drawing blood, checking their noses, eyes, feet and mouths. Big animals must be **sedated** to be examined. No lion willingly lets you check to see if his teeth are in good shape! Our goal is to keep our animals well, so we don't have to do emergency operations very often.

Conclusion

Creating the perfect zoo is both a big job and a serious responsibility. Some people don't like zoos. They feel they are cruel and believe all animals deserve to be free. The best zoos, however, serve several important purposes. They provide visitors with entertainment but are also places where scientists can study animals. Through careful breeding, endangered species may be saved from extinction. Zoos can help us connect more closely with nature. They also encourage us to love, respect and care for all the living creatures that share our planet.

These newborn giant panda triplets were born at a zoo. They are being kept in an incubator until they grow stronger.

Glossary

architect a person who designs buildings and other structures

aviary a place where birds are kept

browse to eat grass and plants

carcasses the bodies of dead animals

carnivores animals that eat other animals

exotic animals animals that come from other parts of the world

herbivores animals that eat only plants

illegally doing something that is not allowed by law

nutritionist someone who is trained to give advice on how food affects an animal's health

omnivores animals that eat both plant food and other animals

primates the group of animals that includes apes and monkeys

sedated put to sleep with medication

Index